King Arthur's

Puzzle Quest

This is a Carlton Book

Published in 2017
by Carlton Books Limited
20 Mortimer Street
London W1T 3JW

ISBN 978-1-85375-963-5

10 9 8 7 6 5 4 3 2 1

Printed in Dubai

King
Arthur's
Puzzle Quest

Puzzles Inspired by the Once and Future King
and his Legendary Quest for the Holy Grail

CARLTON
BOOKS

4

Contents

The Quest Begins

Welcome to Albion, o valiant one! You have entered a land of heroic knights, scheming wizards and ancient riddles. The fact that you have obtained this mystical tome proves your worthiness to join the greatest quest of all: the search for the Holy Grail. Along the way you will meet Arthur, the One True King of Albion, and his retinue of fearless warriors, the Knights of the Round Table. You will also encounter some of the king's enemies, who will try to confound you with tests of logic and lateral thinking. Only the most intrepid knight can hope to find the Grail, but courage alone will not suffice. You will need a mind as keen as Excalibur's blade to navigate the tangled forest of puzzles and conundrums that stand between you and your prize.

Good luck and God's speed, brave knight! The fate of Albion is in your hands.

Part One

The Making of a King

Uther

After months of brutality and bloodshed, the war was finally over and the land had its One True King: Uther Pendragon. He stood in the window of his tower, waiting for the dawn. He had not slept one wink.

When the sun appeared on the cloud-strewn horizon, the new Overlord of Britain fancied that it looked like a fresh blood stain. Was it a portent of short-lived peace?

There was a quiet cough from the doorway and Uther turned to see his counsellor, Merlin the Wise.

"The lords await your pleasure, sire," said Merlin.

Uther growled. Meeting these men in battle was one thing, but he struggled with the rules of diplomacy.

Sensing his reluctance, Merlin asked:

"What is the thing that you may give to everyone, and yet still keep?"

What is the answer to this riddle?

SOLUTION ON PAGE 106

Igraine

As peace settled on the kingdom, the battle-weary nation turned its thoughts to gentler pursuits. King Uther was no exception.

Gerlois, the Duke of Tintagel, had died leaving a widow, Igraine, and two young daughters. Igraine was an incredibly beautiful woman and she drew the attention of the new king.

Uther spoke to Merlin of his feelings every day, asking if there was some enchantment the wise man might employ to make Igraine love him.

One morning Merlin snapped and asked the king:

"What is as small as a cooking pot, yet all the oceans in the world could never hope to fill it?"

SOLUTION ON PAGE 106

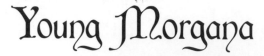

Young Morgana

Igraine had two daughters from her previous marriage: Margaise and Morgana le Fay.

Even as a child, Morgana was a strange creature. She created several wicked enchantments in the form of puzzles. See if you can solve this one. Apparently, if you fail to solve it, you'll be transformed into an earthworm.

1. You must trace a line that passes through all the obects without taking your quill from the page.

2. You may not enter the same square twice.

3. If the line passes through a lake (splash), it must immediately change direction, left or right, on that square.

4. If the line enters a forest (leaf), it must turn left or right at the next empty square.

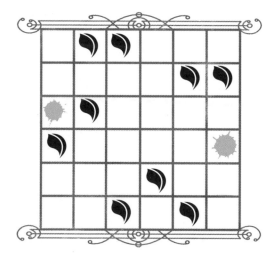

Solution on Page 107

A Dark Prophecy

In the tenth year of their marriage, Igraine bore Uther a son. Merlin was present at the birth and dismissed the midwife with a cold and meaningful stare.

"What is it, Merlin?" asked Uther.

"My liege, I bring a grave portent. Your life draws to an end, and your infant son is in danger."

Uther rose. "Do more enemies come? Must I ready my armies for battle so soon after this moment of happiness?"

"Nay, sire. The enemy that comes cannot be fought with sword or lance. I speak of the Death that ravages the towns and villages of your kingdom."

Uther's eyes were wide with fear. "Is there nothing that can be done?"

"I can save the boy, sire."

Uther's panic turned to impotent rage. "You have brought this plague upon us, wizard! You have angered God with your enchantments." Merlin looked the king in the eye and the monarch's words froze on his tongue.

> *"Your majesty, to give me to someone I don't belong to is cowardly, yet to take me when I do not belong to you is noble. What am I?"*

SOLUTION ON PAGE 107

The Realm in Ruins

As Merlin had prophesied, the plague came to the house of Uther. Before he died, the king charged Merlin and Sir Ulfius to take his son to safety.

With the passing of Uther, the kingdom fell into chaos once more.
  Shade and label each region of the map to show which king controls which regions. No two neighbouring regions are controlled by the same king.

King Mark = KM

King Ryence = KR

King Leodegrance = KL

Find out which king occupies the castle and which two kings are laying siege to it.

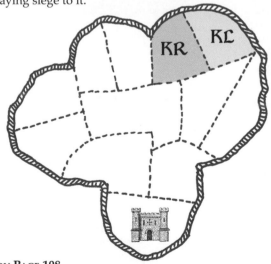

SOLUTION ON PAGE 108

A King Will Come

Having taken Uther's son beyond the reach of war and pestilence, Merlin went to visit the archbishop.

The kingdom's chief cleric looked distraught. "Will we ever know peace, Merlin?"

"A new king will rise, your grace. Even now he sleeps, untroubled by the affairs of men. But ... he is coming."

"But how will the kingdom know this man?" asked the archbishop.

"I will devise a test that only the true king may pass," said Merlin.

The archbishop looked sceptical, but Merlin continued:

> *"Before he died, Uther gave something to the new king. It is a possession that others in this realm will make more use of than the king himself."*

SOLUTION ON PAGE 108

The Brothers

Some years later, Merlin's test of kingship was constructed at the Great Cathedral. It consisted of a huge stone, on top of which was mounted an iron anvil. Into the anvil, apparently in defiance of any natural law, a steel sword had been thrust.

Beneath the anvil, a golden plaque declared:

Whoever pulls this sword from the anvil, he shall be the One True King of Britain.

The archbishop announced a tournament that would decide which knights and noble lords were worthy to take the test.

One lord who heeded the call was Sir Ector. He came with his two sons: Sir Kay, who had already established himself on the tournament field; and Arthur, who was acting as squire to his older brother.

"I've never seen so many knights in one place," whistled Kay. "There must be almost a hundred."

"Slightly more," said Arthur, "I've counted 678 legs and 452 eyes."

How many knights are there?

SOLUTION ON PAGE 108

A Gathering of Lords

Over the course of the day, the number of knights competing to draw the sword was whittled down as men were unhorsed and had to be helped from the field by their squires.

Ten tourneys were fought by the noble lords. Can you work out how many tourneys each has won?

King Ban of Benoic

King Lot of Orkney

King Ryence of North Wales

King Pellinore of the Isles

Find the value of each king's shield from the grid below. The numbers are the sum of the shields' value in that column or row.

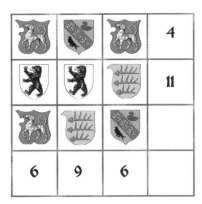

SOLUTION ON PAGE 109

The Tournament

The tournament challengers met in earnest.
This was no friendly contest since the prize
was no less than the kingdom itself!

Sir Kay's first joust pitted him against the fearsome giant Sir
Balamorgineas. Kay fought with a desperate courage and struck the
massive knight's helmet with such force that his blade shattered.

When the two warriors disengaged, Kay asked Arthur to find him
a replacement sword.

After the first day there were 60 wounded knights. Thirty-seven
had sustained injuries while on horseback and 47 had been hurt
while fighting on foot.

How many poor knights had been injured twice, both in the
saddle and out of it?

Solution on Page 109

Drawing the Sword

A rthur found himself at the door of the Great Cathedral and, beside him, the Test of Kings – the great stone, the iron anvil and ... the sword!

Without thinking, Arthur reached for the hilt of the sword, but froze when he noticed that the enchanter Merlin was standing beneath the great arch.

"I, I was ..." Arthur stammered.

Merlin simply smiled. It seemed to Arthur that the distant clamour of the tournament, the crowd, even the birdsong in the nearby wood were drowned out by the deafening sound of his own heart beating. After an eternity, Merlin spoke:

"What will you break the very moment you say its name?"

Solution on Page 109

Lost in the Crowd

Kay was pacing impatiently. His combat with Sir Balamorgineas had been declared null and void, and he needed to find another opponent, or he would forfeit the competition.

"Did you find a sword?" he asked when Arthur returned.

"I did," said Arthur, handing the bright steel blade to his brother.

Kay's eyes widened. The sword was a master-crafted weapon, a thing of beauty with an edge as keen as winter. It was, unmistakably, the Sword of the One True King.

"But … how?" was all he could manage, then some strange impulse seized him and he quickly wrapped the sword under his cloak before running off without a word.

Arthur was left in a whirl of noise as the melee continued. Kay had disappeared into a crowd of seemingly identical knights. Can you find his shield among the others?

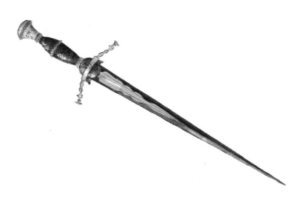

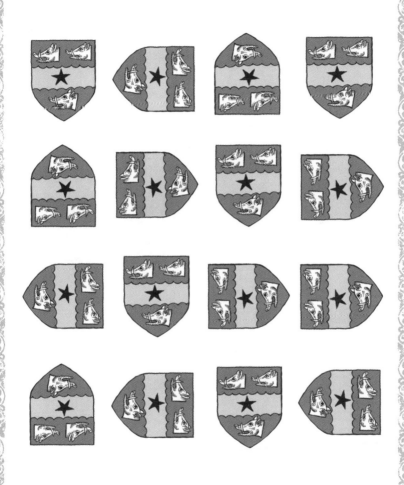

SOLUTION ON PAGE 110

Hidden Swords

There are nine swords hidden in the picture. Can you find them all?

A Squire's Last Errand

hen Sir Ector saw the sword, his first question was whether Kay had pulled it from the anvil.

Kay's expression was conflicted, but his knightly honour won out and he admitted: "No, Arthur did."

Sir Ector looked at his youngest son and seemed to be on the verge of making an important pronouncement, but instead he said: "You must put it back!"

The knight and his sons made their way back to the Great Cathedral, but their hopes of returning the sword without drawing attention were utterly dashed; a huge crowd had gathered around the now-empty anvil. As they arrived, Merlin raised his hands and the crowd was instantly hushed.

Arthur walked forward under the unwavering gaze of Merlin. The wizard had another riddle for the boy. In a low voice that only Arthur could hear, he asked:

"What is it that becomes larger the more you take away?"

Solution on Page 112

Bloodline

Arthur rejoined his father and brother with every king in the land scrutinizing his every move.

"I beg your forgiveness, father," said Arthur. "I should never have taken the sword. I've brought dishonour on our house."

"You are not my son," said Sir Ector, his voice half-choked.

Tears of shame welled up in Arthur's eyes and he bowed his head.

"Oh, no!" Ector clasped the young squire's shoulders. "Arthur, it's the truth. I am not your father. Merlin brought you to me when you were still a baby."

"But who is my father?"

Can you find the name of Arthur's father in this chaos of letters?

HRETTOUUTHREUOEROTOTRUTTH
OTHERUTHUHTURTTORTHEROTOT
THUTHERUTTHRETTOUUTHREUTU
THERUTHRETTOUTORTHEROUTHU
UTTORTHEROTOTRUTTHRETTOUUT
ETTOUUTHREUTUTHOTHERUTTHR
HEROTOTRUTTHRETETTOUUTHREU
RUTHUHTURRUTHUHTURHEROTO

SOLUTION ON PAGE 112

The Lords are Humbled

One by one, the other lords stepped forward to take the test. All thoughts of organized competition were forgotten and things quickly turned violent.

The archbishop tried to appeal for calm, but he was rudely pushed aside and his mitre was knocked from his balding head.

Merlin watched as the squabbling knights, lords and kings jostled for position before they too tried and failed to pull the sword from the anvil.

And then a lone voice shouted from the crowd: "Let the boy try!"

It was uncertain whether it was a peasant or a noble who started it, but soon the whole crowd seemed to have taken up the cry.

Arthur was pushed forward. Once again he put his hand to the hilt and drew the sword from the anvil in one clean motion. The roar of the crowd was deafening.

"SILENCE!" shouted Merlin, and his voice was like an avalanche followed by a wintery hush.

> *"Give him food and he shall thrive. Give him water and he shall perish. Tell me ... who is he?"*

Solution on Page 113

For or Against?

A violent argument broke out immediately. Some lords were happy to bend their knee to the new king, but others were still convinced that Merlin had tricked them.

The value of each shield is how many supporters (including themselves) each king has. The numbers show the sums of the columns and rows. If the corresponding king has an odd number, he has turned that many nobles against Arthur. If his number is even, he has brought that many lords to fight for the young king. Can you work out how many enemies, and allies, Arthur has?

King Mark

King Leodegrance

King Urien

King Pellinore

SOLUTION ON PAGE 113

Castle Defenders

You are spying for King Arthur and must find out where the enemy's defences are. Every castle has at least one knight on a neighbouring square to its north, south, east or west.

No knight can be in a neighbouring square to another knight, not even diagonally. The numbers tell you how many knights are in that row or column. Can you work out where all the knights are located?

		♜				♜		2
								0
♜	⚔						♜	2
				♜				0
		♜			♜			3
						♜		0
		♜				⚔		2
					♜			1
0	3	0	1	2	0	3	1	

Coronation Day

Merlin and the archbishop agreed that no time should be wasted in anointing the new king.

Arthur was reluctant to accept, given that so much of the kingdom was still in chaos, but Merlin finally persuaded him that the kingdom could be healed only by one who was king in both name and deed.

The coronation took place at the Great Cathedral. This time it was the archbishop who offered Arthur a riddle. "I expect it will not be long before I see you in this holy place again," he said with a wink.

"Your grace?" asked the new king, who was starting to wish that his advisors would speak plainly.

"What binds two, yet touches only one."

Solution on Page 114

Messenger

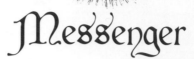

A rthur met with his warlords and they grimly assessed a ragged map of the kingdom. The kings loyal to Arthur were horribly outnumbered, yet they fought on fiercely.

"I must know how the other lords fare," said Arthur. "We must get a messenger to King Leodegrance and see if Cameliard still holds."

Sir Kay stepped forward. "You cannot entrust this mission to a squire, my king. The roads are crawling with enemy forces. I will go."

Sir Ector asked, "Do you know what you are undertaking, my son? Only half of the messages we send reach their destination."

"I'm not afraid of Urien's cut-throats, father," Kay replied. What are the chances of the brave Sir Kay completing his mission?

SOLUTION ON PAGE 115

The Battle of Bedegraine

A rthur was now officially the High King. But there were still eight rebel lords who contested his legitimacy. In the forest of Bedegraine, a last desperate battle would be fought. Arthur would need to deploy his forces wisely in order to emerge victorious.

Each one of the enemy kings 👑 must be countered with a knight ♞ on a neighbouring square to its north, south, east or west.

   No knight can be in a neighbouring square to another knight, not even diagonally. The numbers tell you how many knights are allowed in that row or column.

	👑			👑	**2**
				👑	**1**
👑			👑		**2**
		👑		👑	**0**
		♞			**3**
👑					**0**
2	**0**	**3**	**0**	**2**	**1**

Solution on Page 115

Part Two

The Sword and the Queen

The Royal Tour

Spring came to the kingdom and Arthur began a tour of the realm with his court.

They were a few hours into their journey when they came to a signpost consisting of five signs pointing to five different castles.

"Ah, so we must follow the road yonder for Tintagel," said Sir Kay, who had not wanted to admit that he was starting to feel lost.

"I fear not," said Merlin. "See how the earth beneath the sign is disturbed? I believe bandits have twisted it to lead unsuspecting travellers into peril."

"So, how are we to find our way to the castle?" asked Sir Kay.

SOLUTION ON PAGE 116

A Wounded Knight

Arthur's court had finished setting up camp in the Forest of Usk when a knight and his squire rode into the clearing. The knight had been severely wounded in combat and was unable to speak, but his squire presented him as Sir Myles of the White Fountain.

The squire explained that they had travelled to a place known as the Valley of Delight. There they met three beautiful maidens who, upon learning that Sir Myles sought renown by some brave adventure, directed him to the nearby castle of the Black Knight.

On the bridge leading to the castle was a black shield and a brass hammer with a sign that proclaimed: Strike this shield at your peril!

"My master struck the shield with the hammer and the Black Knight came from his castle. He demanded that my master surrender his shield. He refused, of course. So the Black Knight struck him down."

Arthur turned to Merlin and asked if he could heal Sir Myles.

Merlin's voice was grave:

"He requires something. The man who invented it did not want it. The man who buys it does not need it. The man who needs it does not know it."
What is it?

SOLUTION ON PAGE 116

Knights Errant

A band of young knights asked Arthur's leave to seek the Valley of Delight and avenge Sir Myles.

However, only half of the knights enlisted the help of an enchantress to locate the magical valley. The remainder were forced to return to court.

When they reached the Valley of Delight, a third of the knights were so distracted by the three maidens that they forgot their quest entirely. Of those that continued to the castle, half were killed in combat with the Black Knight. Only two knights returned with their lives, but without their shields.

How many knights had set out on the quest?

SOLUTION ON PAGE 117

Morgana's Guidance

W here is this Valley of Delight?" the king demanded. "I will find the Black Knight myself and bring him to justice."

"He can be found only by magic," said Arthur's half-sister Morgana, with a strange smile. "I can show you the way, but first you must solve my puzzle."

She presented the king with one of her maps and a quill pen, and reminded him of the rules:

1. You must trace a line that passes through all the objects without taking your quill from the page.

2. You may not enter the same square twice.

3. If the line passes through a lake (splash), it must immediately change direction, left or right, on that square.

4. If the line enters a forest (leaf), it must turn left or right at the next empty square.

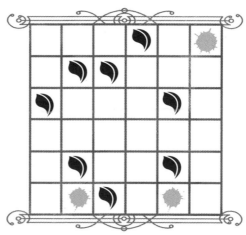

SOLUTION ON PAGE 117

Three Maidens

After making his way through the Enchanted Forest, Arthur came to a beautiful valley. It was exactly as Sir Myles' page had described, complete with the three beautiful maidens who were dancing among the flowers.

"You should know, sire, that these maidens are neither mortal nor subject to the laws of civilized discourse," said Merlin. "One maiden only ever tells lies, the other always tells the truth and the third changes according to her whim."

"How can I know which is which?" asked Arthur.

"You must ask one of them for directions."

The first maiden approached and said, "I am not the truthful one."

The second laughed, "But I am not the liar."

The third said, "And I am not fickle."

Which maiden must Arthur ask for directions to the Black Knight's castle?

39

SOLUTION ON PAGE 118

The Tree of Shields

Following the third maiden's directions, Arthur and Merlin came to a bridge that crossed a violent river. Across the bridge was a large tree, from which hung the shields of defeated knights.

Find the value of each shield from the grid below. The numbers give the sum of the row or column. Each liege lord also has a number, so you will then be able to work out which shield belongs to which king.

King Pellinore = 1, King Ban = 2, King Ryence = 3, King Lot = 4, King Urien = 5

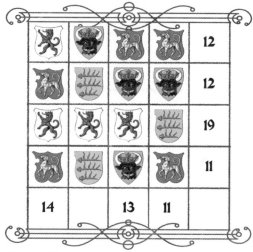

The Black Knight

On the bridge was a black shield and beside it a bronze hammer with the warning: Strike this shield at your peril! Ignoring the warning, Arthur soon found himself face to face with the dreaded Black Knight.

The Black Knight attacked three times before Arthur could respond. In the first two attacks, Arthur's strategy was exactly equal to the Black Knight's. On the third attack, the Black Knight advanced recklessly while cutting and thrusting. How many times did Arthur **dodge** to exactly balance the Black Knight's attack?

Advance	Lunge	Thrust	Cut	Feint

Retreat	Dodge	Riposte	Parry	Taunt

There are five strategies, consisting of an attack and a defence. Each strategy has a shade or pattern and a number (**1**, **2**, **3**, **4** or **5**). You will need to work out which number goes with which strategy.

Black Knight   **Arthur**

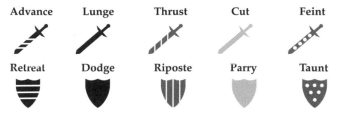

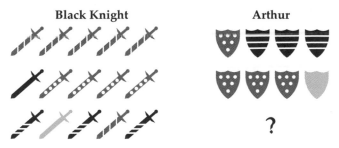

?

SOLUTION ON PAGE 119

An Enemy Revealed

Arthur and the Black Knight fought like possessed men, trading blows with a fury that would have pulverized lesser warriors.

The king delivered a mighty cut to the Black Knight's helmet, powerful enough to break the visor. But in doing so, he shattered the Sword of the One True King!

Arthur's eyes widened as he finally recognized the face of his foe. It was the last thing he saw before he slipped into unconsciousness.

Only one of the names below is a true anagram of the Black Knight's identity. You might need to look at some of the previous puzzles to acquaint yourselves with the knights of the realm.

1. wag wane
2. lip nor len
3. prole line
4. budo bear
5. lance latte

SOLUTION ON PAGE 119

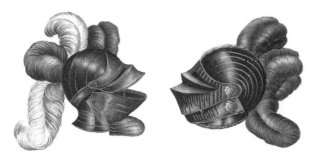

Merlin's Intervention

The Black Knight was grievously injured but, seeing that Arthur was now helpless, he moved in to finish him. Merlin strode forward, waving his staff.

"Stop! You are about to slay Arthur, your true king!"

The Black Knight raised his sword and snarled, "So much the better. Vengeance shall be mine at last!"

Before he could strike, Merlin brought up his staff and tapped him smartly on the back. The Black Knight collapsed in a heap.

"Is ... is he dead?" asked Arthur groggily.

"No, sire, he sleeps."

"That was badly done, Merlin. You struck down a knight who had bested me in a fair fight."

"Things are not always as they seem, particularly when our vision is warped by steel," said Merlin. *"Tell me, sire, is four quarters of a kingdom greater than three quarters?"*

"Yes, of course."

"By how much is it greater?"

"Damn your riddles, Merlin! By a quarter, obviously."

"Really, sire?" asked the wizard with a smile.

SOLUTION ON PAGE 120

A Visitor

Merlin helped the wounded Arthur into the forest, where they came upon a hermit's hut.

The king's condition was graver than he knew; the Black Knight had dealt him injuries that should have been fatal. Merlin marvelled at the young king's will to live.

As Arthur lay in a dreadful delirium, clinging doggedly to life, a royal entourage visited the hermit's hut. It was Lady Guinevere of Cameliard, who had come to buy some herbs. When she saw the injured Arthur, she called for her personal physician.

Together the wizard, the herbalist, the physician and the noble lady tended the young king's wounds and against all hope were able to pull him back from the brink of death.

Soon after Guinevere had departed, Arthur was sitting up and eating a broth that the hermit had prepared for him.

"This is the best soup I have ever eaten, Merlin," Arthur declared. "I have never tasted anything like it!"

The wizard smiled.

> *"You use a blade to slice my head and weep beside me when I am dead. What am I?"*

Solution on Page 120

The Forest of Arroy

When Arthur had fully recovered, he and Merlin returned to court. The king could think of nothing but challenging the Black Knight to a rematch and insisted that Merlin help him find a blade that could replace the Sword of the One True King.

To Merlin's surprise, it was Morgana who proposed a solution.

"Follow my enchanted puzzle, brother. It will guide you through the Forest of Arroy and lead you to what you seek."

1. You must trace a line that passes through all the objects without taking your quill from the page.

2. You may not enter the same square twice.

3. If the line passes through a lake (splash), it must immediately change direction, left or right, on that square.

4. If the line enters a forest (leaf), it must turn left or right at the next empty square.

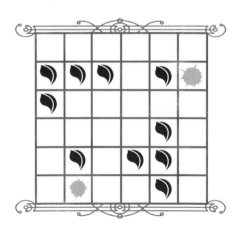

SOLUTION ON PAGE 121

The Lady of the Lake

After solving Morgana's puzzle, Arthur journeyed through the Forest of Arroy and found a circular lake about 100 yards in diameter. On its bank was a boat without sail or oars.

As he approached, something emerged from the very centre of the lake. It appeared to be a woman's arm, holding aloft a magnificent sword.

"None shall move the sword from her hand, except the One True King," intoned Merlin.

"Well, the boat is useless without oars," said Arthur. "It seems I must swim."

"Any mortal flesh that touches the water will wither and die, sire."

"Oh. I don't suppose *you* could–"

"Wizards and water do not mix well, sire," sniffed Merlin. "I did, however, bring this rope. I believe it is just over one hundred yards in length."

Arthur looked at the treeless bank and wondered, not for the first time, if Merlin was slightly mad.

How can Arthur get to the centre of the lake and retrieve the sword?

SOLUTION ON PAGE 121

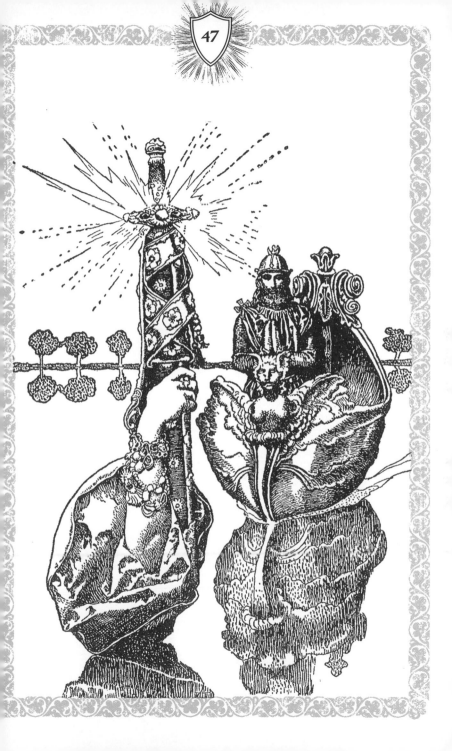

Vindication

Now armed with the sword Excalibur, Arthur returned to the castle of the Black Knight.

After striking the black shield with the brass hammer, he once again confronted the aggrieved King Pellinore, who had recovered from the injuries sustained in their previous engagement.

This time, the combat was decisive: Arthur's sword was like a bolt of lightning, while Pellinore's mightiest blows had no effect on the young king at all. Pellinore was soon forced to yield.

Arthur was merciful and promised to restore his opponent's lands if he would swear allegiance to him. Pellinore gratefully agreed.

Afterwards, Merlin asked Arthur which he valued more: the magical sword, or the enchanted sheath which had protected him from harm. Arthur replied without hesitation that he valued the sword.

Looking slightly disappointed, Merlin asked:

"A bottle of the kingdom's finest wine costs 100 coins. If the wine is worth 90 coins more than the bottle, what is the value of the bottle?"

SOLUTION ON PAGE 122

A Call for Help

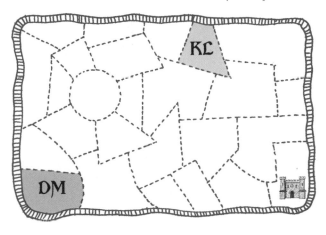

Arthur had scarcely been back in court a week when a herald arrived from Cameliard. The land of King Leodegrance was once again under attack.

The map above shows the areas controlled by the forces of **King Leodegrance** (KL), **King Ryence** (KR) and **Duke Mordaunt** (DM). Label each region so that no adjacent regions are controlled by the same ruler. Whose army now controls the castle at Cameliard?

SOLUTION ON PAGE 122

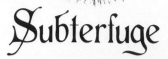

Subterfuge

A rthur wanted to see the threat to Cameliard for himself and decided that the best way to do so was from within the castle.

"This has nothing to do with a certain Lady Guinevere of Cameliard?" asked Merlin.

"I just think I can learn more from the common people than from their warlords," said Arthur, blushing slightly.

Merlin thought the plan was dangerous, but he could not argue with the king's logic and so he gave Arthur an enchanted cap that would transform his appearance.

When he prepared for the journey to Cameliard, Arthur put on the cap and, suddenly, where once a mighty king used to be there now stood a low-born serf.

Merlin smiled grimly and his parting words, as usual, came in the form of a riddle:

> *"I'm the part of the bird that's not in the sky, I'm seen in the water but always seem dry."*

SOLUTION ON PAGE 123

Who is the Fool?

In his magical peasant disguise, Arthur found work as an apprentice to a gardener.

The gardener was a spiteful man who liked to mistreat those he considered to be socially inferior. He particularly liked to pick on a homeless old man who could be found begging close to the royal gardens every morning.

"Look at this fool," said the gardener as he and Arthur approached the old man.

The gardener produced five coins – one silver and four coppers – and said, "Ho, old man. I have a mind to be charitable. Which would you prefer: this silver coin or the handful of coppers?"

The old man pointed at the copper coins with a grateful grin.

The gardener handed over the coins, giving a lascivious wink to a group of giggling ladies who were watching the spectacle. The gardener was almost crying with mirth as he and his apprentice continued on their way.

"Silly old fool, the silver coin is worth ten coppers!"

"I don't think he's the fool," said Arthur under his breath. Why?

Solution on Page 123

The White Champion

After spending some time as a gardener's apprentice at Cameliard, Arthur learned that Duke Mordaunt had designs on the Lady Guinevere.

The duke had challenged any other potential suitors to single combat, declaring that if no champion came forward he would claim his bride by default.

This was too much for Arthur. Casting off his magical disguise, he commissioned a suit of brilliant white armour from a merchant. Then the mysterious 'White Champion' challenged the arrogant duke.

"Choose your weapon, whelp!" bellowed Duke Mordaunt.
Arthur smiled as he recalled one of Merlin's silly riddles:

"I am a common weapon, mercilessly biting flesh and bone.
I have a dove's complexion, but my softness has been crushed.
I am called to war every year, though rarely deployed in anger.
What am I?"

SOLUTION ON PAGE 123

Another War

As the "White Champion", Arthur jousted with Duke Mordaunt and bested him easily. However, the Duke refused to relinquish his claim on Guinevere. Arthur revealed his identity and asked for Guinevere's hand in marriage. The Duke's response was predictable: war!

There are five types of soldier. You must work out the number rating of each – 1, 2, 3, 4 and 5.

Spearmen   Swordsmen   Crossbowmen   Longbows   Knights

Arthur was determined to meet the forces of Mordaunt's ally King Ryence in a fair fight. They fought three battles in total, with the following army compositions. How many spearmen did Arthur field in the last battle to keep the odds even?

King Ryence   **Arthur**

SOLUTION ON PAGE 124

Victory at Camelot

ind the value of each shield from the grid below to work out how many battles each lord won in the war against King Ryence.

King Lot

King Urien

King Pellinore

King Leodegrance

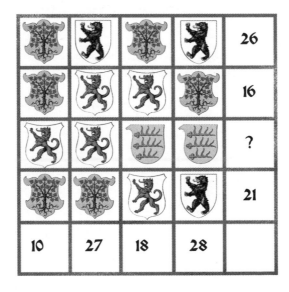

SOLUTION ON PAGE 124

The Wedding

And so King Arthur and the beautiful Lady Guinevere were joined together in holy matrimony.

Merlin gave his blessing in his inimitable style:

"I am the ruler that heads of state must heed.
Unseen, I labour night and day.
Even if you break me, I shall not cease.
One arrow stops me, another enslaves me.
If you lose me, nothing will matter ...
What am I?"

SOLUTION ON PAGE 125

Part Three

Darkness Comes to Camelot

Peace Interrupted

$\mathcal{S}$ir Kay burst into the workshop in a state of desperation.

"Merlin!" he called. "I need a skin of water, quickly."

But Merlin was nowhere to be seen. Kay looked vainly around the cluttered room.

"Dammit, man, I'm supposed to be competing in an archery tournament and I–"

At that moment the wizard appeared, seemingly out of thin air. He was wearing a black hooded cloak and a mask fashioned from the skull of a goat. He laughed and the sound was like a ghostly echo.

Kay let out a shrill scream and fled out the door.

Later that day, Sir Kay sent Merlin a pouch of silver coins and a note thanking him. He had won the tournament.

Can you explain these strange goings-on?

SOLUTION ON PAGE 126

Invasion

I n Arthur's kingdom, peace was precious and fleeting. Shortly after Guinevere's coronation an invading army appeared.

Each one of the enemy lords 👑 must be countered with a knight ♞ on a neighbouring square to its north, south, east or west. No knight can be in a neighbouring square to another knight, not even diagonally.

The numbers tell you how many knights are allowed in that row or column.

			👑				0
							3
👑		👑				👑	0
			👑		👑		3
👑				👑			0
						👑	2
	👑						2
			👑			👑	2
2	1	1	1	1	3	0	3

SOLUTION ON PAGE 126

New Knights

Eight knights of the Round Table perished in the battle with the invaders. It was decided that their replacements should be four veteran knights and four young knights.

There were five young contenders to fill the four places. Each knight was given a number:

**Sir Marvaise = 4, Sir Lionel = 5, Sir Cadar = 6
Sir Baudemagus = 7, Sir Tor = 9**

From the grid below you can work out the value of each knight's shield. The numbers are the sum of each row and column. Can you work out who was not invited to sit at the Round Table?

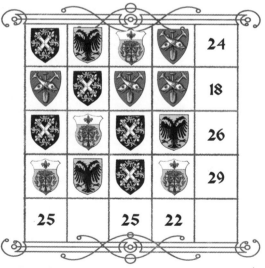

SOLUTION ON PAGE 127

A Lady Scorned

Unfortunately, the knight who was not invited to sit at the Round Table was the son of Morgana. She took his exclusion as a personal affront.

From the king's tower, Merlin watched her storm across the courtyard, taking her entourage from the castle without leave. With a sigh, he turned from the window to Arthur, who was still oblivious to his sister's fury.

"I fear that darkness comes to Camelot, my liege," said Merlin.

"What new evil afflicts us?" asked Arthur.

Merlin thought for a moment. Arthur saw only the best in his subjects and could not believe that those close to him were capable of betrayal. So he said:

> "What comes once in a minute, twice in a moment, but never in a thousand years?"

SOLUTION ON PAGE 127

Vivien

A visitor came to Camelot - a young woman of noble bearing and exquisite beauty by the name of Vivien. She was accompanied by a dwarf servant carrying a silk cushion, on which was presented a flawless ruby set in a ring of gold.

"I present this gift to the wisest member of your court," she said.

The king was invited to try the ring first, but it seemed to shrink at his touch and would not fit on his finger. Other noble lords tried but were equally unsuccessful.

Finally, the lady Vivien presented the ring to Merlin, who had shied away from the ring.

He expressed great reluctance but Arthur, delighting in the wizard's uncharacteristic bashfulness, insisted that he try it on.

Sure enough, the ring was a perfect fit. Merlin endured the laughter of the court for as long as he could, then tried to remove the ring. But it was stuck fast!

"The ring acknowledges you as the wisest man in the realm, my lord," said Vivien sweetly, "Please wear it, for my sake. I have a riddle for you:

I am lighter than a feather, warmer than ice, cooler than flame. Yet the strongest man can't hold me for much more than a minute. What am I?"

SOLUTION ON PAGE 128

A Wicked Plot

"Did the wizard accept the ring?" asked Morgana.

"He did," said Vivien. "He was reluctant, but even he could not refuse a royal decree."

"And now no sorcery on earth can remove it," chuckled Morgana as she handed Vivien something that glistened brightly in the twilight. "The ruby ring he wears is twinned with this diamond one; while you wear it, the old man will be your abject slave."

Vivien smiled brightly, "He will teach me all his sorcerous skills, and when I have nothing left to learn, I shall neutralize his power forever."

Morgana laughed. "My brother the king will be furious if any harm comes to his pet wizard."

A sly frown twisted Vivien's beautiful face. She said:

"Just last week there was a bloody death in my father's realm. The magistrate found a dagger belonging to my brother. The blade was covered in the victim's blood, but no charges were ever brought against my brother. Do you know why?"

SOLUTION ON PAGE 128

All's Fair

Arthur gave Vivien leave to attend her brother's funeral. There she met a handsome young lord, who was very courteous towards her.

After the guests had departed, she could not stop thinking about the young man. She had to see him again, but no one seemed to know who he was.

Vivien described the man in great detail to her sister Evangeline, but all she received in reply was a fit of sobbing.

Apparently taking pity on her sister, whose grief was clearly greater than her own, Vivien handed her a goblet of wine.

This seemed to calm Evangeline slightly. "I'm so sorry, Vivien. I really have no idea who the young man might be ..."

Her eyes bulged with sudden panic. She tried to speak, but red foam frothed from her lips.

Vivien watched with indifference as the poisoned wine did its work and her sister died painfully at her feet. Can you explain the motive behind Vivien's evil act?

SOLUTION ON PAGE 128

The Castle in the Valley

Merlin was granted leave to travel with the Lady Vivien, although he could not recall where he had agreed to take her.

After they had ridden for several miles, they stopped in a glade not far from the Valley of Delight to get their bearings. Vivien produced a curious map, which seemed all too familiar.

"There is a castle in the valley where you can complete my education," said Vivien. "We must simply decipher this enchantment to find it."

1. You must trace a line that passes through all the objects without taking your quill from the page.

2. You may not enter the same square twice.

3. If the line passes through a lake (splash), it must immediately change direction, left or right, on that square.

4. If the line enters a forest (leaf), it must turn left or right at the next empty square.

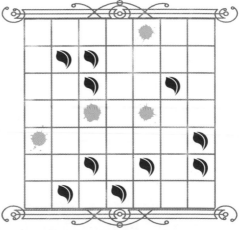

Mendacious Maidens

As Vivien had predicted, they came to a castle in the Valley of Delight that rivalled Camelot in its grandeur.

Five beautiful maidens greeted them at the gatehouse.

"Finally!" said Vivien with a cruel smile. "Merlin, let me introduce my handmaidens: Alicia, Beatrice, Camille, Daphne and Eleanor. They are fay and do not speak as mortals do. Each will tell you three things: two truths and a lie."

As they entered the courtyard, Merlin was horrified to see a knight lying face down in the mud with a knife between his shoulder blades.

"Who did this?" croaked the wizard.

"It was not me!" said Alicia. "I've never stabbed anyone. Daphne did it!"

"I am innocent," said Beatrice. "The poor boy was stabbed. But I know it wasn't Daphne!"

"I did not do this," said Camille. "The blade belongs to Eleanor. Daphne is surely the killer!"

"It wasn't me!" said Daphne. "Alicia accused me falsely. It was Eleanor!"

Eleanor said, "I am blameless, I've never seen that dagger before. Beatrice did it!"

Which of the handmaids murdered the knight?

SOLUTION ON PAGE 129

Merlin's Doom

Once the wisest being ever to walk the land of Albion, Merlin had succumbed to Morgana's magic and Vivien's wicked charms. He was little more than a puppet, but deep inside he raged against his own gullibility.

Now that she had extracted the last of his secrets, Vivien prepared to neutralize the wizard forever. Kneeling before him she said sweetly, "Dearest mentor, you seem fraught. See, I have prepared this soothing draught for you. Drink and be at peace."

As he drained the poisoned chalice, Merlin became lucid for an instant and uttered a final riddle:

> *"What is the thing the entire world waits for? A source of hope for some and dread for others. We wait in vain, because it will never come. And yet, we wait."*

SOLUTION ON PAGE 130

A Gift

Morgana returned to Camelot with an air of humility that no one believed for an instant.

No one, that is, except Arthur. He was so glad to see his half-sister that he immediately forgave her earlier discourtesy.

As a token of her contrition, Morgana presented the king with a beautiful black horse. It was the finest destrier he had ever seen.

The two scions of Uther Pendragon went out riding the following morning.

"I have a wager for you, brother," said Morgana. "A race through yonder forest."

Arthur laughed. "A wager I'd gladly take, sister. But it seems unfair; your generous gift is surely the swiftest horse in the kingdom, whereas your own is little more than a dray."

"Indeed," said Morgana, "but I had neglected one important detail. The rider whose horse comes last will win the race."

"Sister, truly you rival our dearly missed Merlin with your enigmas! How would such a race be possible?"

How can Arthur win the race?

SOLUTION ON PAGE 130

Morgana's Path

After riding Morgana's horse deep into the wood, Arthur realized that he was completely lost.

On impulse, he reached into the saddle bag, remembering that the horse belonged to his sister. The pack was empty except for a vellum scroll, onto which was inscribed one of Morgana's puzzles.

1. You must trace a line that passes through all the objects without taking your quill from the page.

2. You may not enter the same square twice.

3. If the line passes through a lake (splash), it must immediately change direction, left or right, on that square.

4. If the line enters a forest (leaf), it must turn left or right at the next empty square.

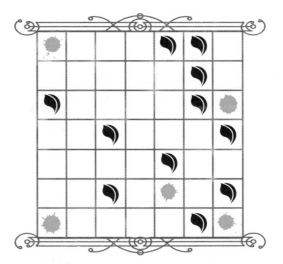

SOLUTION ON PAGE 131

The Dungeon of Sir Domas

A strange sleepiness came over Arthur. Too late, he realized that he had fallen under an enchantment.

He regained consciousness in a dank dungeon cell, lit by fading daylight from a window some fifteen feet up the wall. He quickly realized all his armour had been taken from him and he thanked God that he had left Excalibur in his sister's safekeeping back at Camelot. As his eyes adjusted to the half-light, he became aware that he was not alone.

His fellow inmate offered a wicked smile that was bereft of sanity.

"I've been digging!" announced the wild man.

Arthur noticed the hole in the dungeon floor and a substantial mound of excavated soil. There seemed to be no tools in the cell. Could the man really have done so much with his bare hands?

"It's taken me just over a week to dig this out," continued the man proudly. "I reckon in a few months my tunnel will be clear of Sir Domas's castle!"

"I don't think we'll have to wait as long as that," said Arthur.

What did the king mean?

SOLUTION ON PAGE 131

Enemies Unknown

A maiden came to the cell and informed Arthur that he would be released if he promised to visit Sir Ontzlake, the brother of his captor. Ontzlake had misappropriated some of Sir Domas's land and Arthur was tasked to recover it. He would be given Domas's own armour and would have to perform the mission incognito.

Arthur agreed, thinking there must be a diplomatic solution to the issue. However, he dispatched a messenger to his sister Morgana, asking her to send him Excalibur.

Some days later the messenger returned from Camelot bearing the sword and its enchanted scabbard.

At the gates of Sir Ontzlake's castle, he was met by a mysterious knight clad all in black. The Black Knight informed Arthur that Sir Ontzlake had been wounded in a tournament and had sent him in his stead. When Arthur suggested that the castle belonged to Sir Domas, the champion roared in anger and drew his sword.

The two warriors clashed with a fury and although Arthur was the better swordsman, he could not land a decisive blow on the Black Knight. By contrast, the knight's blows pierced Arthur's armour in several places and he bled fiercely. With a flurry of savage cuts, he disarmed the king and knocked him to the ground. The Black Knight stood ready to deliver the killing blow, but first he spoke:

"I am to give you a message from Queen Morgana."

Arthur lifted his visor. "Morgana, my sister?"

The Black Knight seemed momentarily stunned when he looked upon Arthur's face. The king did not hesitate but sprang up and wrestled the sword from his hand. Impossibly it looked like his own sword, Excalibur.

Falling to his knees, the Black Knight removed his helmet and Arthur was shocked to see the face of Sir Accalon, one of his own champions.

"What was the message?" asked Arthur, scarcely able to believe what had befallen.

"He who has it doesn't tell it. He who takes it doesn't know it. He who knows it doesn't want it. What is it?"

SOLUTION ON PAGE 132

Justice

Arthur had been thrice deceived. Not only had he been tricked into fighting one of his own knights with a counterfeit Excalibur, but he soon discovered that it was the wicked Sir Domas who had deprived his brother Ontzlake and others of their inheritance. Arthur's justice was swift; he confiscated Domas's lands and divided them among the true claimants.

Divide the land below into four regions of the same shape, so that each has one of the following:

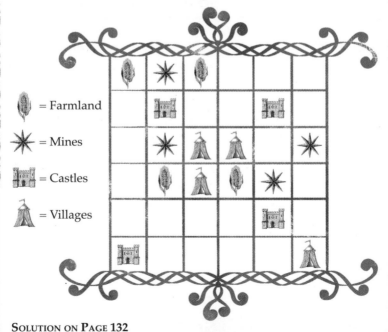

= Farmland

= Mines

= Castles

= Villages

SOLUTION ON PAGE 132

Morgana Goes to Ground

Morgana's final act of vengeance was to steal the magical scabbard that imbued Arthur with invincibility. She fled to the Forest of Arroy and cast it into the lake.

Arthur and his knights pursued her into the forest but arrived too late. Morgana had cast a spell that transformed herself and her entourage into a circle of standing stones, putting them beyond the King's justice. As a parting shot, the vengeful lady had left one of her enchantments on a scroll. On it she had simply written:

Solve me or perish.

1. You must trace a line that passes through all the objects without taking your quill from the page.

2. You may not enter the same square twice.

3. If the line passes through the mud (splash), it must immediately change direction, left or right, on that square.

4. If the line enters a forest (leaf), it must turn left or right at the next empty square.

SOLUTION ON PAGE 133

Sir Pellias

§ir Pellias was an exemplary knight whose brave deeds earned him the title "the Gentle".

On a Mayday ride near the enchanted woodland known as the Forest of Arroy, Sir Pellias met a maiden who was greatly distressed because her husband had been imprisoned in the castle of the Red Knight. The brave Sir Pellias did not hesitate to offer his services. However, he had not come out suitably attired for battle and the ride back to Camelot to retrieve his armour would waste valuable time.

He knelt in a grove and offered up a prayer for guidance. The Lady of the Lake appeared to him in a ray of sunlight and said: "There is a fay smith in the forest who can fashion armour without fire or hammer."

"I shall seek out this smith," said Sir Pellias, "although it is strange indeed that they require no forge."

The Lady of the Lake smiled and said:

"What goes round the wood but never enters the wood?"

SOLUTION ON PAGE 133

The Red Knight

After a lengthy joust and many thunderous clash of lances, Sir Pellias agreed to fight the Red Knight by sword, a more intimate form of combat. This was a duel to the death ...

The Red Knight rained down a savage flurry of four slashes, followed by a thrust, but Sir Pellias defended by parrying three times. He then countered with an even more furious storm of steel: three slashes, two thrusts and then two more slashes for good measure. The Red Knight was able to defend by parrying four times.

The Red Knight then swung his sword in a single slash to Pellias's head and followed with four desperate thrusts. How many times did Sir Pellias have to parry the attack?

There are three strategies: slash, thrust and parry. You will need to work out the numerical value of each strategy. Each attack must be answered with a defence that is exactly equal.

SOLUTION ON PAGE 133

Freeing the Prisoners

After defeating the Red Knight, Sir Pellias released the knights who had been held captive in his dungeon. Some prisoners had died in captivity, so once again there was the issue of dividing up misappropriated land.

Divide the land below into four regions of the same shape, so that each has one of the following:

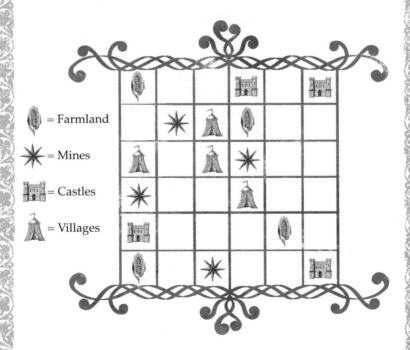

= Farmland

= Mines

= Castles

= Villages

SOLUTION ON PAGE 134

The Green Knight

Sir Pellias's next battle was against Sir Engamore, otherwise known as "the Green Knight".

The Green Knight attacked tentatively with a slash and two thrusts, and Pellias defended himself by parrying twice. Then Pellias unleashed a flurry of three slashes and two thrusts, which forced the Green Knight to defend himself with three parries. This drove the Green Knight into a frenzy; his sword became a whirling blur of death, and he slashed and thrust four times each.

How many times did Pellias have to parry to defend himself?

There are three strategies: slash, thrust and parry. You will need to work out the numerical value of each strategy. Each attack must be answered with a defence that is exactly equal.

Solution on Page 134

Part Four

Knights of the Round Table

Camelot's Champion

The Lady of the Lake herself appointed
Camelot's newest and greatest champion;
he was Launcelot, son of King Ban of Benwick.
Launcelot was much loved by the court, and
especially the Queen. But his spirit had been
touched by the fay, so he felt at peace only when
he roamed the world and slept beneath the stars.

One day before departing on another solitary quest, the Queen
asked him if he ever felt lonely. Launcelot replied:

"I have four companions:
One runs but never tires.
The second eats but is ever hungry.
The third drinks but is ever thirsty.
The fourth fills a room but is never seen."

"Who are these remarkable
comrades-in-arms?" asked the Queen.

SOLUTION ON PAGE 135

Under an Apple Tree

Upon hearing that Camelot had a new champion, Morgana was determined to find him and do him some mischief to spite her brother. Using sorcery, she found Launcelot asleep beneath an apple tree.

He had been dreaming of his adopted mother, the Lady of the Lake. Throughout his childhood, she had honed his mind with wondrous riddles.

Morgana magically transformed herself into the likeness of the Lady, and whispered into the slumbering knight's ear:

> *"You do not want me. But when you have me, you do not want to lose me. What am I?"*

Solution on Page 135

Evil Enchantment

Launcelot had received the blessing of the Lady of the Lake. This protected him from Morgana's malign sorcery but did not prevent the enchantress from taking him back to Castle Chateaubras and holding him captive.

There are nine five-pointed stars hidden in the picture below. Can you find them all?

SOLUTION ON PAGE 136

Morgana's Captive

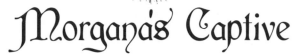

Morgana presented Launcelot with one of the mystical puzzle maps, confident that he had no experience with her arcane traps.

1. You must trace a line that passes through all the objects without taking your quill from the page.

2. You may not enter the same square twice.

3. If the line passes through a lake (splash), it must immediately change direction, left or right, on that square.

4. If the line enters a forest (leaf), it must turn left or right at the next empty square.

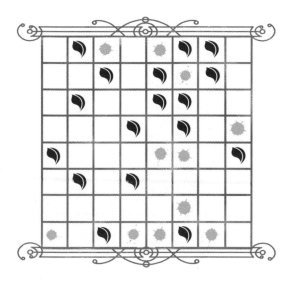

Solution on Page 137

Elouise the Fair

Launcelot was released from Morgana's enchanted castle by Elouise the Fair. In return he promised to aid her father King Bagdemagus in a tournament against the King of Wales.

Some of the segments on the opposite page do not belong to the picture below. Can you find which?

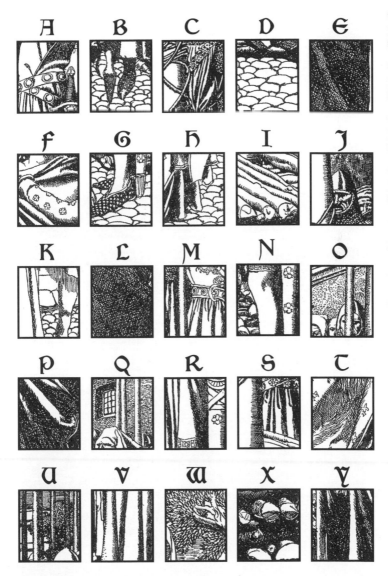

Solution on Page 137

Treacherous Turquine

hile travelling the land as a knight errant, Launcelot encountered the treacherous Sir Turquine, one of the most deadly knights he had ever fought.

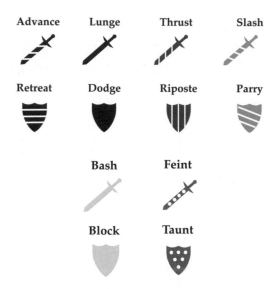

In each of the following six paragraphs below, the strategies of both sides are perfectly balanced. Can you work out the value of each strategy?

There are six strategies, each consisting of an attack and defence. The attack and defence in each category have the same number value (so advance is worth the same as retreat, etc.).

1. Launcelot opened the combat quickly with a thrust that Turquine only just managed to dodge. Turquine angrily thrust and then slashed twice at empty air as Launcelot taunted him.

2. Launcelot taunted the furious Turquine again, making the enraged knight advance with an ineffectual slash followed by an equally off-target thrust.

3. Turquine lunged, then bashed Launcelot with his shield. Launcelot retreated and feinted, which forced Turquine to dodge. Turquine attacked wildly and missed. Launcelot countered the clumsy slash with a riposte.

4. Turquine lunged desperately and Launcelot was forced to retreat twice to avoid being run through.

5. Launcelot advanced, thrust and slashed as Turquine taunted him, then slashed again, which Turquine barely managed to block with his shield. Turquine tried to regain the initiative by lunging, but Launcelot parried and riposted. Turquine slashed out in desperation and Launcelot took a nimble step back.

6. Turquine was now in a frenzy. He slashed and lunged, then slashed and lunged again. Launcelot was able to hold back the storm of steel by blocking just once with his shield, then he riposted…

SOLUTION ON PAGE 138

Liberation

After defeating Sir Turquine, Launcelot liberated many noble prisoners from his castle.

Divide the land below into four regions of the same shape, so that each has one of the following:

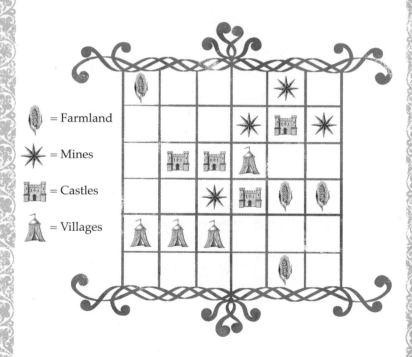

= Farmland

= Mines

= Castles

= Villages

The Plague

Portents of doom had started to spread across the kingdom and, to give further weight to the people's fears, the plague returned.

The total death toll from the plague doubled each day. On the first day it had killed one person; by the second day it had claimed two; by the third day, four; by the fourth, eight. On the fifteenth day, it had wiped out the entire population of a village. How long would it have taken the village to succumb to its fate if the plague had claimed two lives on the first day?

Solution on Page 139

Dark Dreams

Prophecies and omens were becoming all too common. The captain of Camelot's men-at-arms knelt before Arthur, trembling.

"Sire, last night the wizard Merlin came to me in a dream!" he said.

Arthur's face creased with grief. He missed Merlin greatly.

The captain continued: "He told me that the spawn of the enchantress would raise a dark host and bring an end to Camelot."

"I thank you for your prophecy, captain," said Arthur. "It saddens me to do so, but I must relieve you of your rank and banish you from Camelot."

The captain cried out in despair, but he offered no protest to the king's punishment.

Why did Arthur treat him so?

SOLUTION ON PAGE 139

The Grail Knights

Arthur realized that something would have to be done to hold back the tide of terror that was sweeping his kingdom. He gathered his greatest knights and charged them with the greatest quest of all: the search for the Holy Grail.

Sir Kay = 2, Sir Mordred = 3, Sir Percival = 4, Sir Gawaine = 6, Sir Pellias = 11, Sir Launcelot =13

From the grid below, you can work out the value of each knight's shield. The numbers are the sum of each row and column.

Can you find which knights were sent on the quest?

				25
				30
				22
16	23	27	38	

SOLUTION ON PAGE 139

Profit or Prophet?

"What have you found?" asked Percival. He watched with some amusement as Sir Kay excitedly excavated soil from beneath the ancient rune-carved dolmen.

"Well, it isn't the Grail," grinned Sir Kay, "but I might be able to retire early!"

He finally produced a mildewed cloth sack from the hole and poured its contents onto the grass: a great pile of silvery coins.

"They're Roman," said Kay proudly. "See here, this is a silver denarius, date stamped 44BC with the head of Gaius Julius Caesar himself!"

Percival looked sceptical. "This is just another trick to distract us from our quest. Put the coins back, Kay. They have no value to us."

Why would Percival think so?

SOLUTION ON PAGE 140

The Blacksmith

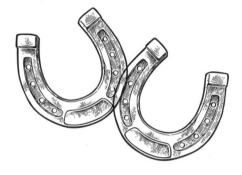

Sir Percival's horse had lost a shoe, so he took her to a smithy in the woods. While he waited, he overheard a strange conversation between the blacksmith and the local abbot.

"How much will one cost?" asked the abbot.
"One piece of copper," said the smith.
"And for five?"
"Two pieces of copper."
"What about twelve?"
"Four copper pieces."
"Very well, I shall take four."
How much will the blacksmith charge the abbot? And what exactly is he buying?

SOLUTION ON PAGE 140

The Enchantress Vanquished

The brave Sir Percival had sworn to vanquish all evil from the Kingdom, no matter what form it took. However, when he confronted the wicked Lady Vivien, she begged for clemency, and his true knight's heart softened.

Instead, he commanded her to release all the knights that she had turned to stone with witchcraft. To which Vivien exclaimed:

"You will need the milk of the cow that is more ancient than mankind but never more than a month old."

What was she talking about?

SOLUTION ON PAGE 140

The Madman in the Woods

I n the Forest of Arroy, Launcelot encountered a hermit who had evidently been driven mad by his prolonged solitude.

However, he claimed to know what Launcelot was seeking on his quest, so the knight listened patiently while the madman sang a tuneless song:

> *"Tis not a bull, but horns it has, Tis swifter than a dead man's mind,*
> *Tis not a mule but bears the load, Home is never hard to find,*
> *Neither wealthy nor a miser, Silver's always left behind."*

What is the hermit singing about?

SOLUTION ON PAGE 141

Divide & Conquer

King Leodegrance and King Pellinore had combined their forces to support King Arthur. The combined army would now have to be split up to fight on four separate battlefields.

Pellinore's archers and knights were better than Leodegrance's, whereas Leodegrance's men-at-arms and lords were superior to Pellinore's. Numbers were assigned to each type of soldier to help grade them. You must divide up the grid below into four equally shaped parts, each containing 40 points of soldiers.

Type of Soldier	Leodegrance		Pellinore	
Peasants		1		1
Archers		2		3
Men-at-arms		5		4
Knights		6		7
Lords		9		8

SOLUTION ON PAGE 141

The Son of Launcelot

A young man came to Camelot and declared that he was Galahad, the son of Launcelot.

King Arthur studied the boy and liked what he saw. He had the noble bearing of his father, tempered with a true knight's humility. He also had a quality that the king could not quite define.

"Oh, how I wish Merlin was here," Arthur thought. "He could always put a word to a feeling."

And then a riddle came to mind, as if from Merlin himself.

Arthur smiled and asked the court:

"What is it that, after you take away the whole, some still remains?"

SOLUTION ON PAGE 142

Galahad's Journey

$\mathcal{S}$ir Galahad began this quest with simple provisions, so strong was his faith that whatever he needed to find the Grail would be provided along the way.

He travelled one third of the journey by river boat, a quarter of it on foot, and the remaining 80 miles on horseback. How far did he travel in total?

The Knight of the Bridge

Galahad at last came to a large stone bridge, which crossed a river of boiling poison. On the other side was a chapel, in which was hidden the object of his quest: the Holy Grail.

In the centre of the bridge was a tollhouse, which a Black Knight had been charged to guard. The Black Knight was protected by the most powerful magic and even the combined might of Arthur, Launcelot and Galahad himself would not have been sufficient to overcome him.

The Black Knight was instructed to come out of the tollhouse every five minutes and turn back anyone attempting to cross the bridge. The monks of the chapel were also subject to this prohibition.

Galahad calculated that it would take at least ten minutes to get from one side of the bridge to the other.

How did he continue his quest?

Solution on Page 142

The True Grail

Finally, Galahad came to the chapel where the Grail had been hidden. But there was still one puzzle to solve.

The chapel contained goblets and chalices of every shape, size and ornamentation. The Grail could be any one of them!

"A drink from the true Grail will refresh the soul and heal all ills," said the abbot who had been charged to maintain the chapel. "But a sip from a false Grail is the deadliest poison."

"No pressure, then," thought Galahad.

The true Grail is hidden among all these false ones. Can you find it?

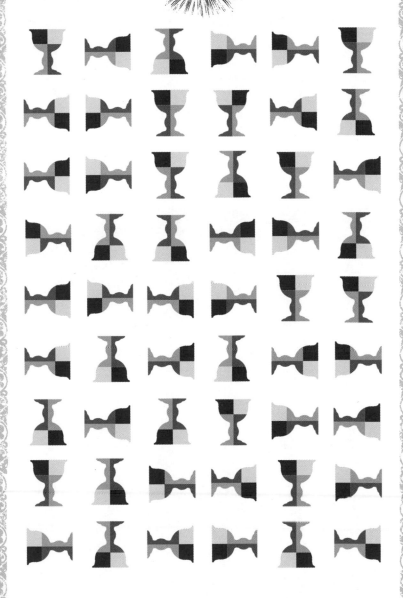

SOLUTION ON PAGE 143

Solutions

106

Part One
The Making of a King

Uther

Your word.

Igraine

"Do you speak of my heart?" asked Uther with a sigh.

"No! A *sieve*, you fool," cackled Merlin,
"although 'your head' might have sufficed."

Young Morgana

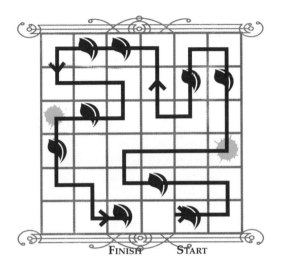

FINISH   START

A Dark Prophecy

Blame.

The Realm in Ruins

The castle belongs to King Leodegrance.

A King Will Come

His name.

The Brothers

If each knight was on horseback, he and his steed would have four eyes and six legs between them. The answer is 113: 678 divided by 6, or 452 divided by 4.

A Gathering of Lords

King Ban won 1 tourney.

King Ryence won 2 tourneys.

King Lot won 3 tourneys.

King Pellinore won 4 tourneys.

The Tournament

Twenty-four knights sustained two injuries. There were 84 injuries in total (37+47) minus 60 knights equals 24.

Drawing the Sword

Silence.

Lost in the Crowd

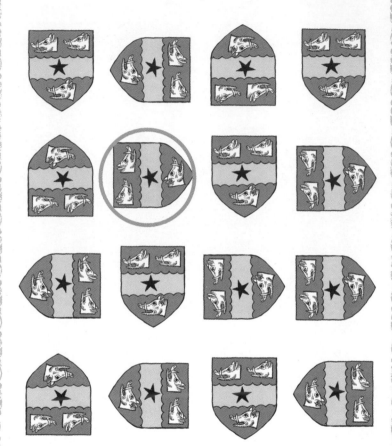

Hidden Swords

A Squire's Last Errand

A hole.

Bloodline

HRETTⵔUUTHREUⵔERⵔTⵔTRUTTH
ⵔTHERUTHUHTURTTⵔRTHERⵔTⵔT
TH**UTHER**UTTHRETTⵔUUTHREUTU
THERUTHRETTⵔUTⵔRTHERⵔUTHU
UTTⵔRTHERⵔTⵔTRUTTHRETTⵔUUT
ETTⵔUUTHREUTUTHⵔTHERUTTHR
HERⵔTⵔTRUTTHRETETTⵔUUTHREU
RUTHUHTURRUTHUHTURHERⵔTⵔ

The Lords are Humbled

"He is fire," said the wizard. "Do not underestimate this tiny spark of a lad, for he shall ignite the flame in all your hearts and bring light to every corner of this benighted kingdom."

For or Against?

King Mark brings only himself (1), Urien brings three and Pellinore, seven. These numbers are odd, so the total number of enemy leaders is 11. Leodegrance brings four who will fight on the side of Arthur.

Castle Defenders

		🏰	⚔			🏰	⚔	**2**
								0
🏰	⚔					⚔	🏰	**2**
			🏰					**0**
	⚔	🏰		⚔	🏰	⚔		**3**
						🏰		**0**
	⚔	🏰				⚔		**2**
				⚔	🏰			**1**
0	**3**	**0**	**1**	**2**	**0**	**3**	**1**	

Coronation Day

A wedding ring.

Messenger

His chances are one in four. There is a one in two chance of getting the message to Leodegrance, then a one in two chance of returning with his reply.

The Battle of Bedegraine

	♛	♞		♞	♛	2
♞			♛			1
♛		♞	♛	♞		2
		♛			♛	0
♞		♞			♞	3
♛						0
2	0	3	0	2	1	

Part Two
The Sword and the Queen

The Royal Tour

By realigning the sign with the correct sign pointing to the castle they had just left, all the other signs would then point true.

A Wounded Knight

Merlin is talking about a coffin.

Knights' Errant

Twelve knights.

Morgana's Guidance

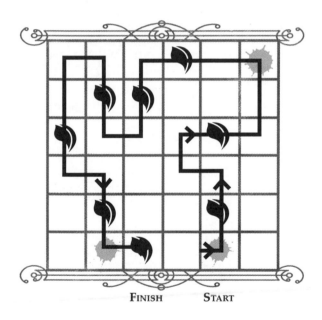

FINISH START

Three Maidens

He should ask the third maiden. The first maiden must be
the fickle one because neither the liar nor the truthful one
can deny being truthful (the liar would be telling the truth
and the truthful one would be lying). The second could be
lying or telling the truth. However, the liar would not be able
to *deny* being the fickle one (since that would be true), which
only leaves the truthful one.

The Tree of Shields

King Pellinore

King Ban

King Ryence

King Lot

King Urien

The Black Knight

The Black Knight's attack is worth 16.

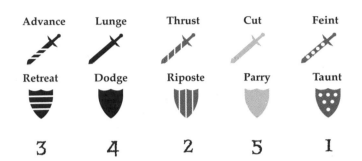

Advance	Lunge	Thrust	Cut	Feint
Retreat	Dodge	Riposte	Parry	Taunt
3	4	2	5	1

So Arthur must dodge four times.

An Enemy Revealed

3, Pellinore.

Merlin's Intervention

The answer is a third.

A Visitor

An onion.

The Forest of Arroy

FINISH   START

The Lady of the Lake

Arthur gave one end of the rope to Merlin. Then, taking the other end, he walked around the bank in a complete circle. When he returned to the wizard, the rope was wrapped around the sword. He then entered the boat and made his way to the middle of the lake by pulling himself along the rope.

Vindication

If the bottle were worth 10, then the value of the
wine would be 100 – 10 = 90 coins. This cannot be right
since that would make a difference between the wine
and bottle costs of 90 –10 = 80 coins.
The correct answer is five coins.

A Call for Help

King Leodegrance still holds Cameliard.

Subterfuge

A reflection, or shadow.

Who is the Fool?

Clearly the gardener enjoyed playing this prank to
entertain the ladies. As long as the beggar continued
to make the 'wrong' choice, he could secure himself a
steady income of copper coins.

The White Champion

A snowball.

Another War

Knights are worth four, crossbowmen are worth five, spearmen are worth three, longbowmen are worth one and swordsmen are worth two. Arthur would need to field three spearmen to make the battle even.

3   2   5   1   4

Victory at Camelot

 King Leodegrance won one battle.

 King Lot won three battles.

 King Urien won seven battles.

 King Pellinore won 12 battles.

The Wedding

Your heart.

Part Three
Darkness Comes to Camelot

Peace Interrupted

Sir Kay had hiccups.

Invasion

				♛				0
♞				♞			♞	3
♛		♛					♛	0
		♞		♛	♞	♛	♞	3
♛					♛			0
♞					♞		♛	2
	♛		♞				♞	2
	♞		♛		♞	♛		2
2	1	1	1	1	3	0	3	

New Knights

Sir Baudemagus, the son of Morgana le Fay,
was not invited.

Sir Marvaise of the Leisle

Sir Lionel

Sir Cadar

Sir Tor

A Lady Scorned

The letter M.

Vivien

A breath.

A Wicked Plot

Vivien's brother killed himself.

All's fair

Vivien thought it likely that her young man might also
attend her sister's funeral.

The Castle in the Valley

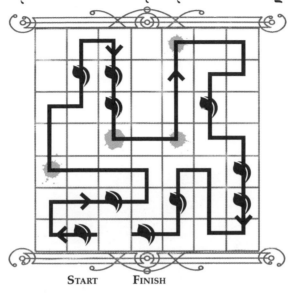

Mendacious Maidens

Alicia's first two statements amount to the same thing
(her innocence) and, since she can only tell one lie, they must both be
true. Therefore, her third statement (Daphne's guilt) is the lie.
Since we now know that she is innocent, Daphne's first two
statements are also true and her third statement
(Eleanor's guilt) is the lie.
Camille also falsely accuses Daphne, which uses up her lie.
This means her assertion of innocence is true, and so is
her statement that the dagger belongs to Eleanor.
Eleanor is therefore lying about having never seen the
dagger before. So her assertion of innocence is true and so is
her accusation. *Beatrice is the murderer.*

Merlin's Doom

"Tomorrow," said Vivien.

A Gift

Arthur and Morgana would simply
have to swap horses.

Morgana's Path

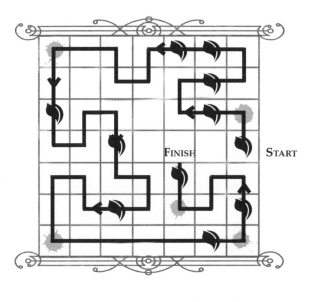

FINISH   START

The Dungeon of Sir Domas

If the man stood on the pile of soil and Arthur
climbed onto his shoulders, they could reach the
window instead.

Enemies Unknown

Counterfeit coins. As Arthur was soon to learn,
Morgana had created forgeries of Excalibur
and its scabbard, and given the originals to the
unwitting Sir Accalon.

Justice

Morgana Goes to Ground

FINISH

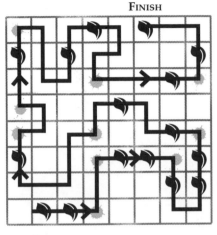

START

Sir Pellias

Tree bark.

The Red Knight

Twice.

Freeing the Prisoners

The Green Knight

Pellias parried five times.

135

Part Four
Knights of the Round Table

Camelot's Champion

The four elements: water, fire, earth and air.

Under an Apple Tree

A law suit.

Evil Enchantment

Morgana's Captive

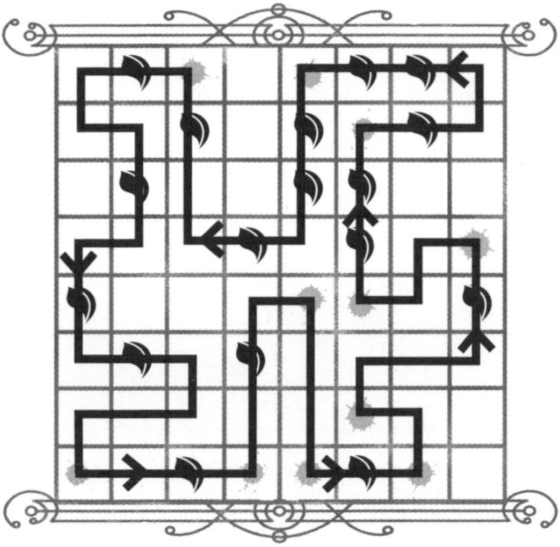

Elouise the Fair

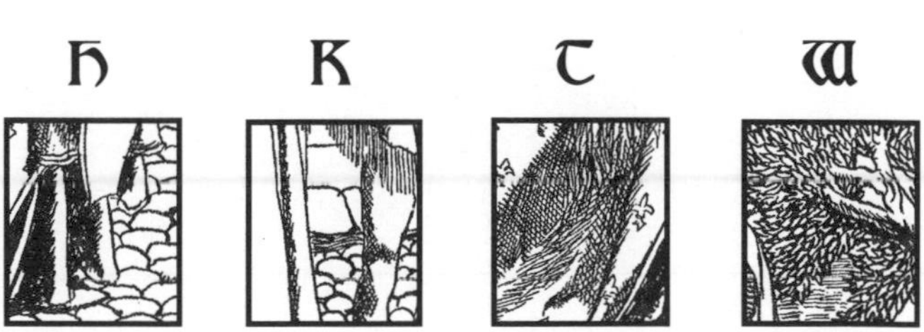

Treacherous Turquine

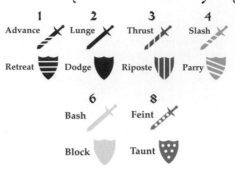

1 Advance

2 Lunge

3 Thrust

4 Slash

Retreat

Dodge

Riposte

Parry

6 Bash

8 Feint

Block

Taunt

Liberation

The Plague

Fourteen days. The progression would have been exactly the same (minus one villager) as if it had started on the second day.

Dark Dreams

The captain was on night watch. He should not have been sleeping last night.

The Grail Knights

Sir Kay, Sir Percival, Sir Gawaine and Sir Launcelot.

Profit or Prophet?

The designation BC (or equivalent) was never used by
the Romans. But, more importantly, no coin minted
before the birth of Jesus of Nazareth would have been
date stamped "Before Christ".

The Blacksmith

The abbot was buying a wrought-iron Roman numeral.
The cost was one copper piece per line.

One (I) costs one, Five (V) costs two, Twelve (XII) costs
four, So Four (IV) would cost three.

The Enchantress' Vanquished

Moonlight.

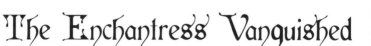

The Madman in the Woods

A snail. Well, it rhymes with Grail.
You should never hope to get helpful information
from a madman in a forest!

Divide & Conquer

The Son of Launcelot

The word "wholesome".

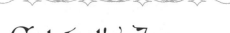

Galahad's Journey

192 miles.

The Knight of the Bridge

Galahad acquired a monk's habit and wore it over his armour. He started across the bridge, but just before he reached the tollhouse, he turned on his heel and headed back in the direction from where he had come. Right on time, the Black Knight came out of the tollhouse and bellowed, "Where do think you're going, brother?" Seizing Galahad by the hood, he redirected him "back" towards the chapel.

The True Grail